Chapter 1:
Introduction
Chapter 2:
Survival and marriage
Chapter 3:
Difficulties of the first marriage
Chapter 4:
The possible solutions to the
marriage problems
Chapter 5:
The types of education for early
marriages
Chapter 6:
The basic soft skills for newly
married couples
Chapter 7:
The hard skills that are needed by
the newly married couples
Chapter 8:
The benefits of marriage survival
Chapter 9:
The A-Z marriage secrets and tips
Wrapping Up:
The permanent solutions for
marriage problems

Foreword

Getting through your first year of marriage when you are another couple can be testing, particularly assuming that you are as yet finding out with regards to the next individual.

For the most part, it is smarter to get to realize somebody prior to getting hitched yet we as a whole realize this isn't the means by which things occur throughout everyday life.

You meet somebody extraordinary who make your day and before you know it, you're overwhelmed with passion for them.

As of now, you've been considering getting hitched and race into things too early.

We've seen it so often before with couples everywhere.

Get all the data you want here.

First Year Marriage Survival Instructions to Survive Your First Year Of Marriage For New Couples

Part 1:
Presentation
Synopsisynopsis On the off chance that you two have not lived respectively yet, there is a decent opportunity that contentions will happen later in the relationship once you all move in together.

We frequently see this much of the time.

It's really alluded to as the "stages" in your relationship.

Every relationship goes through a phase, regardless of the fact that you are so near the individual.

You may be finicky individual who inclines toward everything perfect while your accomplice simply tosses his trash any place he is standing.

Different issues might emerge like times for closeness, burning the midnight oil, going out with companions, and how you handle business around the house.

These things can add to how you two get along.

Rules ought to be laid out with the goal that way you both can live joyfully hitched.

The Basics Marriage isn't simply attempting to get by.

It is more significant then that. Marriage is tied in with making penances for the one that you really love.

Whenever they are debilitated, you make time away from work to deal with them.

Assuming that your accomplice is disturbed with regards to you going out a ton and not focusing on them, you should give them a greater amount of your time.

Doing little things can be a major assistance and make the relationship less sensational in the feeling of contentions.

Ensure you let your mate in on the amount they mean to you every day and never take them from rock.

No one can tell when you will see them again and to this end it's so significant.

Relational abilities are one of the main parts of marriage.

On the off chance that you can't speak with your other a large portion of, the relationship is ill-fated.

Have a go at talking less and listening more.

Or then again assuming you are somebody who talks more and listens less, the time has come to listen carefully.

Perhaps your companion needs you to pay attention to them so that way you'll know precisely the way in which they feel about a specific circumstance.

Part 2:

chapter 2:

Endurance and marriage Abstract

Abstract To endure marriage, you want to know what your needs are first.

Work ought to never be your main goal, in spite of the fact that your folks could say so in any case.

Your mate should start things out all the time.

All things considered, they are the individual that imparts the home to you, prepares dinners, brings in additional cash for your both, helps watch the children, and be close every once in a while.

Getting by There is such countless exercises to do in marriage and in this age, generally the two individuals are working.

This makes the marriage so troublesome on the grounds that men are not used to doing exercises that a lady would do.

For instance, most men will not press their clothing or clean the washroom. It truly isn't something they would do. Furthermore neglect establishing blossoms out in the terrace. They will not go close to the blossoms.

Men are prepared to really buckle down by their dads and get a well-rounded schooling to accommodate their loved ones. They aren't the ones who can become pregnant and develop near their kid.

Ordinarily, when the mother has conceived an offspring is the point at which they become passionate.
 A man needs to see their kid to trust the truth of the matter.
 They're not sure what ladies go through during pregnancy and anticipate that we should do everything around the house.
Lady are by and large more passionate and appear to talk more than accomplishing family work.
 Assuming the latrine spills or the sink is broken, think about who they call? They call their better half in a frenzy.
The lady are great at taking care of errands like collapsing clothing, preparing a flavorful dinner, and getting looking good for that dance their significant other is taking them to after work.
Ultimately, toward the day's end - both man and lady are in a similar bed. The lady is perusing her book, zeroed in eagerly on what

she is perusing.

The man can thing around a certain something and that is sexual closeness. This is the main time he starts to converse with her, trying sentiment and in any event, scouring her.

At times it works and now and then it doesn't. At the point when men do get as they

would prefer, they as a rule get on top and take care of their business. Later, their life partner simply lies there, attempting to pause and rest.

The issue is that the man as of now nods off without saying I love you or anything that shows appreciation.

It is like nothing at any point occurred.

Clearly, this is on the grounds that most men aren't passionate and they simply do things at whatever point they like.

Isolating ordinary exercises and attempting to get to know each other on an enthusiastic or actual level can challenge.

Right now, therefore couples are going directly toward separate.

 This is on the grounds that they don't have any idea how to impart and be reasonable for their mate.

 It just takes participation, tuning in, and a little sympathy with regards to the next individual.

Part 3:

Troubles of the primary marriage

Synopsisynopsis

There are numerous troubles with regards to marriage.

 The most well known are assumptions, closeness, association and cash.

These points can add to an issue.

 The spouse might burn through huge load of cash on his betting propensities while the wife is disturbed and simply needs him to stop.

 They need that cash for their youngsters.

Another model is for the lady.

 She is frequently too occupied with getting things done around the house that she ends up being anxious and sex is the keep going thing at the forefront of her thoughts.

In any case, the spouse profoundly esteems closeness and without it, he might feel as though he is becoming separated from his significant other.
Difficulties
Every one of the seemingly insignificant details will amount to make a couple begin contending.
They might be angry toward each other and not have any desire to figure out things with one another.

Some might attempt yet once in a while the other individual isn't however helpful as they seem to be. This makes connections so troublesome.

Here are the four challenges with regards to marriage:
Assumptions The spouse has such exclusive requirements for you when you return home.

She doesn't need you to leave your towel on the floor and furthermore won't allow you to eat in your own room, out of dread that there will be scraps on the bed.

This doesn't make you excited by any means.

Concerning you, you anticipate that your significant other should constantly eat prepared when you get back home and to put her best self forward.

This is all you truly care about. Closeness Assuming that you've been wanting closeness for half a month and your significant other is too worn out to even consider doing anything with you, it is essential to see how he feels. Rather than constraining him, give him a delicate backrub that shows you give it a second thought.

He might be under a ton of stress from work.

With regards to closeness, it works the two different ways for people.

Association

Interfacing with your other half is vital.

Assuming you two have a profound association, there is no space for separate or a split up.

Most couples who are associated with one another will more often than not comprehend each other better.

Compassion and sympathy in the relationship go connected at the hip.

On the off chance that their accomplice is tragic, they are.

At times it might require a couple of years for a couple to feel really associated with one another or under a couple of months, contingent upon how lengthy they've been together.

Cash Unfortunately, monetary issues are one of the top purposes behind separate.

On the off chance that you two experience difficulty dealing with cash and bills will more often than not stack up, the relationship will become stressed.

It is stressed on account of the pressure that is gathered during monetary difficulties.

Section 4:

The potential answers for the marriage issues

Synopsisynopsis

Being hitched has many advantages and assuming you stay together to figure out on issues that emerge, the relationship will develop further.

Remember that both of you will need to chip away at marriage issues.

Provided that one individual will go to mentoring or converse with you about the issues of the marriage, it will be a single direction road. This implies the marriage will not have the option to advance.

It is critical to tell your other half why you need specific propensities in the relationship to change.

Tell him/her you are not kidding and in the event that things don't change, that you might just petition for legal separation.

Your mate will see that you are talking business and will need to change a portion of their propensities.
 Obviously - don't be astonished on the off chance that when you two plunk down, they talk about a portion of the things you do.
 It is additionally alright for them to address your negative quirks when you it comes to marriage.

Arrangements are genuinely simple to think of in a marriage yet adhering to those arrangements isn't simple 100% of the time.
 This is what you two should survive and on the off chance that one of you experiences difficulty adhering to your objectives, correspondence is vital.
The other individual could come to the real world and told you they can't change, despite the fact that they have attempted.
 Certain individuals are at a spot in their lives where they truly don't have any desire to change.

Something should fuel their powerful urge to change. More often than not, this want is to keep you and improve their everyday life.

You ought to comprehend that with conceivable marriage arrangements, only one out of every odd thought you think of will work.

For instance, assuming you choose to have separate financial balances due to your better half's ways of managing money - she could even implore you to get her cash.

Yet again this makes pressure on the marriage, since you see her propensities unfurling and this prompts a contention.

Perhaps it's not the spouse this time. Your better half regularly visits boorish strip clubs and leaves you at home.

His reason is that you never get physically involved with him. Tell him it isn't affirm to do this and the following time he gets it done, you should leave for a couple of days.

When you return, center around the closeness in your relationship.
Are you too drained to ever be close with
him? Zero in on his necessities prior, before you both hit the hay.
 Make it fun and don't carry on like it's an errand.
 We bet that the both of you partook in one another when you initially entered the relationship, correct? By taking him back to this time, he will see the value in you and remain at home on a more regular basis.
 On the off chance that he doesn't, it could be an ideal opportunity to release it as this truly wasn't his reason to go out.
Part 5:
The kinds of training for early relationships
Synopsisynopsis
Do you know the kinds of training for early relationships? There are around five phases of marriage where several becomes more acquainted with one

another, deal with issues, contend, move past these issues, center around kids, and become effective in their marriage.

Most of the time, this will require numerous years.

In any case, a few couples are honored at every turn.

They were companions for so long that they know the propensities for their life partner and never again need to work at the marriage.

Everything appears to wake up without anyone else.

Whenever this occurs, it is an obvious that you two are firmly fortified.

Training

Presently, assuming that you are encountering relationship issues, you might be in the beginning phase of "reality".

At this stage, you are simply getting to know how they act in specific circumstances.

You might see your significant other or spouse at their most awful when they are furious or vexed.

This can be an alarming circumstance, particularly on the off chance that you have not seen these sorts of feelings from your accomplice previously.

A large part of the time, this will cause contentions not too far off.

How about we feel free to take a gander at a portion of the sorts of training for early relationships and how each stage unfurls:

The Honeymoon Stage - Almost generally in the special first night stage, couples are very amped up for each other and the sentiment appears to simply take off all alone.

This is on the grounds that they aren't encountering any issues throughout everyday life.

Most couples take part for no particular reason sexual exercises with each other and will likewise appreciate luxuriating in sentiment.

This is when couples go out for supper with one another, activity together, and show up for parties together.

The special first night stage can either be before the wedding or after it, on their vacation.

It truly relies upon the time allotment you've known the individual.

Reality Stage - At this stage, a few couples feel lost and will even contrast their accomplices and a previous sweetheart or sweetheart.

They start to feel that the relationship is an error and they probably won't be viable with that individual.

Sensations of misery, disillusionment and even indignation can surface.

This is totally typical and the motivation behind why couples go through this is on the grounds that issues are beginning to top through.

Whenever a couple is exceptionally close with each other, they'll frequently see the "awful" attributes of that individual.

This leaves the other individual troubled and uncertain of how to treat the relationship.

More often than not.

Ordinarily, the truth stage keeps going as of recently.

Family Stage - The connections turns out to be nearer in childbearing years because of a portion of the contentions that may region.

Rather than the attention being on the actual marriage, everything is coordinated toward the children.

The man and lady work more diligently to arrive at their objectives, rather than going out on a heartfelt date.

They understand that arranging a family includes a ton of arrangement.

When they have a youngster together, they'll turn out to be nearer as a team to attempt to satisfy their kid.

Issues, for example, the child crying, clinic visits, and monetary issues might emerge right now yet at this point - you both will know how to deal with it once the truth stage as passed.

The achievement stage-If you two have been together for a very long time or more, there is a decent opportunity you have finished the achievement stage.

Typically when your kids become a young person or a grown-up, you've gone through all that there is to go through perhaps in a marriage.

Most would agree you have observed a daily existence accomplice where you two will be there until the end. Congrats!

Part 6:

The fundamental delicate abilities for recently wedded couples

Synopsisynopsis

Could it be said that you are recently hitched and need to realize the fundamental delicate abilities you'll require to advance through the marriage? To do this, you can't ask a lot from your accomplice and openness is absolutely vital.

Tolerating your accomplice how she/he acts is vital.

You can constantly discuss any negative quirks or conduct later, yet delay until directing.

For the present, it's better for the both of you to battle once in for a spell and deal with irritating parents in law.

Assuming that there are beyond a few issues, you can address them at the same time.

Abilities

Love

The main thing that keeps a relationship intact is genuine love for the other individual.

In the event that you love them for their character rather, what they resemble, there is a decent opportunity you two will go far throughout everyday life.

Your significant other could be a staggeringly stunning looking lady and later become greater due to the last two kids she favored you with.

In another occasion, you totally revere your attractive spouse yet something has completely changed him.

He was as of late assaulted by a bear, leaving him scarred all over.

You two developed nearer and despite the fact that he has scars all over and some distortion, you actually love him for his character.

He's forever been an entertaining and active person.

Give him bunches of affection and like that he's still near.

Recollect that is assault might have been extreme to the point that it would have been deadly.

What's in store Anything that you do, it's anything but smart to bother on your accomplice or expect excessively. This can be incredibly unpleasant on them.

It is smarter to support them and give them ideas now.

By doing this, you will assist them with developing personally and foster better propensities.

On the off chance that your person was untidy before he even met you, there may have been a few little changes. Rather than tossing his jacket on the floor - he gets it.

This is clearly a characteristic of progress however don't anticipate that he should clean the entire house or do clothing.

Correspondence
Conversing with your life partner is vital.
 On the off chance that you two can't examine significant issues, issues, or dates inside the relationship - consider the marriage over.
You could in any case be in the truth phase of your marriage and for this situation, you are simply getting to realize that your accomplice is exceptionally timid around individuals. In the event that he is modest around you, give him a slight push.
You'll have to do this by asking him inquiries and looking at anything that rings a bell.
 On schedule, he'll come around so do whatever it takes not to stress such a great amount over it.
The hard abilities that are required by the recently hitched couples
Synopsisynopsis
Marriage can be something delightful yet consolidating hard abilities into another marriage isn't something that everybody needs to do.

Be that as it may, you should do this to ensure the marriage advances.
In the event that you don't, the marriage will be ill-fated and you'll essentially have nothing to work with.
Recall that Earth was made for people to interface with one another and a large portion of our life rotates around family recollections.
This is totally valuable to us.
Family should start things out 100% of the time as opposed to going out with companions, working excessively, or worrying about little things that don't have any bearing towards the relationship.
Go slowly and partake in your time.
Continuously be uncompromising with your accomplice by joining hard abilities into the relationship.
The following are a couple of you'll need to find out about:
Hard Skills
Critical thinking
At the point when you two need to go eat out, it is a consistent fight.

For instance, he appreciates eating food from South America while you simply prefer to eat sushi.

He totally loathes sushi and anything with fish or rice with soy sauce isn't something he might want to eat.

This leaves you feeling troubled when it's at last an ideal opportunity to eat out.

What about going to two distinct cafés to get what both of you need? You can arrange take out and go eat it at home, or plan a heartfelt supper at the recreation area.

To eat at a genuine café however, simply carry your food with you that you purchased from the other eatery.

You two will be blissful and won't contend any longer with this kind of procedure.

As may be obvious, critical thinking in a marriage is vital.

Put your life partner first

This is likely the most troublesome thing to do since a large portion of us are for the most part childish creatures.

Be that as it may, assuming you love your life partner - you ought to do this for them.

Discover what they need.

You can constantly account for your requirements on an alternate day.

Assuming that they are feeling anxious, miserable, or irate - talk with them.

Inquire as to whether you can effectively make he/she feel good.

They will begin to foster more regard toward you.

Be a forgiver

Commonly seeing someone, the spouse or husband accomplishes something wrong that disturbs the others. This leaves sensations of frustration, outrage, despair or even misery.

Keep your sentiments down and converse with them concerning why they did what they did.

Assuming it is an issue with cheating, you'll have to know why they did this to you.

Commonly when individuals cheat, their companion isn't giving them what they need.

The most obvious explanation is for absence of closeness or absence of feelings.

Individuals will have a passionate or actual illicit relationship, contingent upon what issues are inside the marriage.

Rather than getting disturbed, just let them in on how harmed you are and you need to make it work.

Allow them somewhere around another opportunity.

The advantages of marriage endurance Synopsisynopsis

Getting through marriage has incredible advantages for couples.

Some of them incorporate developing personally, become really adoring, having the option to communicate your issues with your other half, and, surprisingly, turning out to be monetarily steady with you two working.

Marriage pledges involve being together everlastingly and you ought to show up for your mate consistently. Thusly, you will end up being an intellectually sound individual and will help them also.

Children can incredibly profit from your marriage as we as a whole realize how outrage treats kids when their folks experience separate.

Help yourself out and don't release them through this.

Taking as much time as is needed to make it work is totally ideal for your future.

Try not to surrender!

The following are a couple of advantages of marriage endurance underneath:

Benefits

Being blissful throughout everyday life

Whenever you are with somebody you genuinely love, you'll turn into a more joyful individual throughout everyday life.

All things considered, they are there to impart giggling to you, perk you up, or go with you in the midst of misery. Assuming you are going for continuous medical clinic visits for malignant growth, you could feel tension yet in the event that your other half is there to help you - you will have a vastly improved day.

This is only one illustration of what we are referring to.

By having an accomplice, you won't go through specific circumstances alone. Sadly, certain individuals who are bereft or as of late separated become unpleasant and cutthroat towards others.

Safeguarding your youngsters

By remaining in your marriage, you are safeguarding your youngsters.

For instance, numerous young ladies who don't have fathers will no doubt become pregnant at a youthful age or fall into a defiant demeanor which could bring about drug use or drinking.

A dad is there to give love, discipline, and insurance to whatever might hurt his girl.

Additionally, a few children will foster sadness subsequent to seeing their folks split up.

Our children are unimaginably valuable and you'll need to ensure they are OK.

 Seeing a child grow up with bitterness in their heart is something that could destroy a parent.

 More often than not, we would do anything for our children to be content.

There is a more prominent possibility of this assuming that they youngsters have seen their folks together for a long time.

It very well might be a befuddling and miserable year for them.

 It doesn't keep going for a year however can scar a kid throughout everyday life.

Turn out to be monetarily steady
For the most part, it takes two individuals to help a family.

Assuming you end up having children, this exacerbates the situation.

A single parent working one occupation will most likely be unable to endure in light of the bills, the expense of a youngster, and shock medical clinic visits.

She could even get expelled from the home due to falling behind.

Nonetheless, with two individuals working - you will turn out to be monetarily steady.

However long the other individual and yourself handle cash well and deal with charges like you ought to, you two will be fine.

Ensure your accomplice doesn't have a betting issue and consistently investigate your financial balance articulations to see what's happening.

No one can really tell when cash could "vanish".

This could be from data fraud or your mate might be taking cash from you for their unfortunate ways of managing money

Sharing a financial balance together ought to just be done whenever you have been together following a couple of years and trust them.

Part 9:

The A-Z marriage privileged insights and tips

Synopsisynopsis

Here are the A-Z marriage insider facts and tips for an effective marriage for recently marries.

Tips

Guidance

Offering guidance to your accomplice in the midst of stress or issues is an incredible method for making the marriage truly work.

Regularly, they won't take out their concerns on you. All things considered, they'll want to open their heart and talk about the issues.

Assuming you can offer your life partner counsel, they'll be thankful that they are with you. Don't have the foggiest idea how to offer guidance? Don't sweat it.

You can constantly give them a backrub and simply hold them.

Ask them more inquiries about the issue to make it appear as though you are truly inspired by the issues they are going through.

Most men would rather not hear everything about their companion's day.

A couple of subtleties are fine however when you over-make it happen, they can become overpowered and won't know what to say.

Commitment

Being dedicated to your accomplice implies seeing them consistently, getting date evenings going, and investing energy regardless of how bustling you are.

On the off chance that you have a little window to be with them on your three day weekend, then, at that point, take the plunge! On the off chance that your adoration is in the medical clinic and hasn't had the option to stroll for a month, visit them regularly.

Present to him/her roses and let them know the amount you love them. Showing your commitment will have them understand the amount you care for themselves and they'll foster a solid bond with you.

These sorts of connections will bloom into something else and they will more often than not keep going for quite a long time at a time.

Genuineness

Assuming you are somebody who is now genuine, this might come simple for you.

Did you host a wild get-together at home and every one of your pals concluded it could be interesting to draw on your white divider? You had no clue about this had occurred, in any event, when you returned home. Your significant other let you know that your child was the person who drew on the dividers. In any case, your child was at the party and taking pictures on his toy camera.

Remember, this camera really processes films for youngsters. In the wake of observing every one of the photos, you feel disheartened in what your better half did.

As you can see here, being straightforward purposes less issues in the relationship - regardless of whether it was your issue.

On the off chance that you can't believe somebody in the relationship, you will constantly be re-thinking their activities to you.

This is clearly not extremely smart for you or your accomplice.

You would rather not blame them for accomplishing something wrong.

Perhaps they did nothing off-base and you are the person who owes them the statement of regret.

See what happens when genuineness isn't inside the relationship? It simply aggravates it.

Closeness

Did you had any idea that closeness and love goes together? While some lady probably won't figure this, men will think about closeness in the bed as a type of adoration.

They accept it is physically recuperating.

Most men become nearer to their spouses in the wake of having intercourse.

Additionally, for lady, foreplay is critical.

Men need to know this as well. Assuming you rush this with your better half, she might feel that you don't adore or like her body.

Take as much time as necessary and have some good times.

You'll partake in the experience more. Giggling Chuckling with your accomplice is fun and even welcomes you both to "play" together.

Recall when you pushed your accomplice in the pool when he was wearing all his garments? He was disturbed at the time yet the both of you chuckled with regards to it later. The photos you took of him with his stunned articulation while falling as just entertaining.

He really wanted to snicker at all that had occurred.

Giving each other tickles and in any event, ridiculing each other is generally an incredible method for placing a grin all over.

Each time you two snicker, you are making recollections that will endure forever.

By giggling, you are driving away anything in your life that is awful. Giggling is a type of mending too. Nurturing Being a decent parent to your kids is vital.

The manner in which you treat your youngsters additionally influences your companion.

Assuming that you are a mother who is extremely focused on the grounds that your children don't pay attention to you, there is a decent opportunity you shout at the children each once and for a spell.

Your better half disapproves of this as

he is an exceptionally quiet and getting man.

Attempt to break down to see how he treats the children are misbehaving.

Gain from him or gain from books on nurturing.

The manner in which you parent your kids will influence them for the remainder of your life and in all honesty - you influence people around you in a chain response.

Wrapping Up

The super durable answers for marriage issues

To observe super durable answers for your marriage, you should begin doing some critical thinking.

There should be an answer for each issue in marriage, for example, cash issues, unfaithfulness, nurturing issues, etc.

Here are a few long-lasting answers for assist you with enduring the marriage:

Focus on yourself

In all honesty however this strategy works.

Ask your accomplice what disturbs them with regards to you and work on that property of yourself. If he/she say's you are excessively bossy, take a stab at quieting down. Do some mind clearing practices and figure out how to get things done all alone.

By doing this, you are setting yourself up for a superior relationship.

You will not depend on what he/she does and can finish a large portion of the stuff.

Try not to expect excessively Whenever you expect a lot from your companion, they will become hopeless in the relationship.

It is potential they will feel angry toward you and this might bring about disloyalty, contentions, or you they could even create some distance from you gradually.

Talk with a guide

Conversing with a guide is superior to squabbling about the littlest issues. Each side can be heard and you will not need to stress over this kind of correspondence exploding into a contention.

The instructor will actually want to turn out a portion of the advancement are acquiring as a team and things might improve then they were previously.

Despite the fact that it might seem like rather a fundamental capacity to work out, it is frequently hard to just verbally speak with one another inside the marriage edge.

 The vast majority find that rather than successful correspondence, they will quite often quibble and this obviously isn't smart for the correspondence practice nor is it really great for the marriage.

 Get all the data you want here.

Your Guide To Amazing Communication

Correspondence Basics

Synopsisynopsis Figuring out how to impart successfully and with no pessimistic meanings or feelings will assist with making an optimal stage for

the two players to be agreeable in.
coming up next are a few successful ways of embracing or now and again keep away from to have the option to lay out some type of viable correspondence inside the relationship:
The Basics
Try not to utilize the brush off or quiet treatment instrument.
This quite often never works and absolutely doesn't help what is happening by any means.
There is certainly a need to talk sooner or later during the present circumstance as a great many people would bear witness to the way that they are truly uncertain with respect to why there is what is going on in any case.
Accordingly by really going out of the way to convey plainly and successfully, the two players will be aware of the genuine reason for the current appalling circumstance and afterward will actually want to push ahead in a useful and positive way.

Figuring out how to speak with deference for one another will be one more vital component to remember for the imparting exercise.

 Offering disagreeable and debasing comments will just contribute adversely to an all around horrendous circumstance.

Thusly in attempting to get the worries across and perceived, there should be a few degree of nobility and regard present in the selection of words utilized.

Attempting to hurt the other party however much as could be expected may appear to be palatable for the development yet it is seldom a decent long haul arrangement and could even harm the relationship unrecoverable.

Invest in some opportunity To Communicate In Person

Abstract

Abstract

Because of the bustling way of life of a great many people it has turned into a fairly typical practice to impart inside the marriage by implies other than genuine verbal correspondence.

This is an exceptionally perilous propensity to shape as in the end the two players will take the time or put forth the attempt to verbally impart by any stretch of the imagination, and this absolutely spells calamity.

Up close and personal Coming up next are a few hints on the best way to approach guaranteeing that verbal correspondence is a crucial piece of the trade inside the limits of a solid and cheerful marriage:

Saving a particular add up to opportunity to zero in on verbal correspondence is at some point exceptionally vital for the couple to have the option to keep up with some degree of closeness through the correspondence work out.

This time distributed offers the two players a chance to express their real thoughts and heart and make each other be perceived in a harmless way.

Doing as such an air that is both inviting and agreeable with next to no interruptions would merit investigating as it will assist with keeping the two players zeroed in on one another and on the thing is being said.

Setting oneself up to have the option to impart in a non contentious way is likewise significant.

Requiring the difficulty and work to be cherishing and sustaining while imparting will urge the two players to be more open to what in particular is being talked about.

Utilizing charming terms and a ton of consolation will likewise assist with working with a superior trade.

Keeping up with the agreeable and adoring verbal trade will consider more things to be achieved.

Listening is additionally important for being completely drenched in the verbal type of correspondence.

Without the capacity to tune in, the two players can not comprehend the

correspondence meeting and neither will any sure result be accomplished. The capacity to just tune in, will obviously recognize the other party.
Check out Body Language
Synopsisynopsis
It is at some point important to have the option to add something extra to the non-verbal communication of the other party to all the more likely get what is happening and how to best arrangement with any surfacing circumstance.
 Figuring out how to peruse the different non-verbal communication signs will likewise permit each party to more readily comprehend and decipher the accomplice's needs and needs and work appropriately to oblige them quite far.
Comprehend
Coming up next are some famous non-verbal communication signs that can be utilized to warn the other party with regards to the current mentality and general attitude of one another:
Eyes cinched shut, firmness in the

neck and shoulders for the most part portray a person who is either vexed or not actually content with something.
These signs can be utilized to successfully assist with stopping what is going on before it leaves hand and to likewise assist with redirecting the individual's regard for something more pleasurable and less disturbing.
This frequently removes the individual encountering cynicism from the culpable circumstance and accordingly uplifting a superior temper.
It should be noticed that not all non-verbal communication signals are negative.
 At the point when an individual is feeling attractive there are additionally a few unpretentious and not so unobtrusive non-verbal communication moves that will permit the other party to react likewise would it be advisable for them they wish to.
This is critical to learn as it will assist with bringing the couple nearer when such shows of non-verbal

communication endeavors are all around read and followed up on. As a rule when the reaction is good, the party utilizing the non-verbal communication abilities to impart will be so supported and blissful, that they would more then likely make it beneficial and pleasurable for the reacting party.

This obviously will elevate the correspondence mode to a more profound and satisfying experience.

To Be A Good Listener
Synopsisynopsis

Figuring out how to be a decent audience surely enjoys its benefits and generally it permits the person to appear to be an exceptionally mindful and chivalrous individual.

This is certainly worth figuring out how to accomplish as a great many people like a decent audience over a decent talker.

Sincerely Hear

Understanding that listening is everything except a latent action is a decent spot to begin.

Nor is listening expected to be an action that is impartial and that's it. Truth be told great audience members can concoct great serviceable arrangements as they can comprehend and follow the different contributing elements to a specific circumstance being examined.

Fostering the ability of having the option to listen cautiously additionally permits the person to "hear" things that are not actually being expressed but then significant enough to require consideration.

Once in a while these implicit pieces of data can be more useful than what is really being said through the discussion, and when these pieces of data permit the pay attention to act in a way that is both calming and supportive to the speaker, a gigantic measure of beneficial outcomes can be capable.

Great audience members are normally individuals who can ultimately become shrewd individuals.

Listening takes a specific degree of restriction and in this way permits the individual to consider the matter being expressed prior to settling on any decisions or giving any reaction.

By basically tuning in, the individual is really permitting the other party to vent everything and anything until completely fulfilled.

After this happens the individual will then, at that point, be more responsive to any counsel or remarks made, accordingly considering some sort of answer for be made.

Two individuals taking and attempting to get the considerations and perspectives across won't in any capacity help what is going on.

Be Clear About What You Say Synopsisynopsis

At some point some unacceptable words are utilized or maybe some unacceptable tone and this can cause what is happening that would some way or another not been approaching. Thusly in the mission all things considered and comprehended, the onus in on the person to be however exact as conceivable with what may be being expressed.

Heads up In some cases it is important to be decisive in both way and selection of words for the person to be viewed in a serious way.

 Without being clearly or inconsiderate, it is feasible to guarantee whatever is being expressed is to be viewed in a serious way and not to be dismissed as immaterial or silly. Being clear in expressing one's necessities and needs is additionally something that ought to be empower inside a sound relationship, as this will offer the two players the chance to learn and regard the alternate's perspective and impression of things. Abstain from getting into the propensity for relying upon individuals figuring out a deeper meaning or expecting one's necessities.

This will no doubt prompt a gigantic measure of dissatisfaction and possible disturbance when things don't go as needs be.

Learning not to apologize for specific sentiments and contemplations is additionally something that ought to be empowered as the people who reliably back down will ultimately not be viewed in a serious way by any means.

Anyway while attempting to impart, it would be fitting to hold all feelings in line and furthermore to talk obviously and immovably without superfluous statures of volume included.

Regard is something vital to get while being clear with regards to what is expected as the people who can't win the admiration of others won't be viewed in a serious way by any means.

In some cases it is important to rehash the solicitation to guarantee the things expressed is appropriately perceived and followed.

This will permit the other party to comprehend the significance of the matter expressed and regard its limits.
Utilizing A Touch While Talking
Synopsisynopsis
Most people should be contacted particularly inside the edges of a sound and cheerful relationship. Without the significant contacting factor continually being worked out, the two players will ultimately feel the missing fixing and this could prompt a few adverse outcomes.
Contact
Contacting and being contacted is something each sound relationship should encounter every day and as much of the time as could be expected. The requirement for contact is extremely basic and essential, and stroking this want will leave the two players feeling esteemed and satisfied. It should be perceived that not all contacting ought to in a perfect world lead to some type of sexual action, as this isn't just compressing yet in addition very superfluous.

The demonstration of contacting ought to basically be practiced as method for conveying love, closeness, solace, bliss and whatever other good implications which are smart for connections.
A caring actual motion can come way and some say farther than the expressed word.
 A many individuals react well to the actual touch as long as there is no sexual undertone to it, except if the touch was explicitly intended to be so.
A great many people are just ignorant about the colossal impacts a basic touch can convey, accordingly frequently committing the genuine error of not consolidating the touch activity into the regular day to day existences inside a relationship.
Most relationships very nearly breakdown will normally agree on the way that there was somewhat no contacting inside the relationship, except if sex was the plan.
This is fairly a pitiful situation, to live with, as contacting says a ton

regarding the sensations of adoration and closeness of the couple inside the relationship.

In any event, while having a basic discussion with the other party, some contacting could be started to help the individual unwind and be more open to what exactly is being said.

The Importance Committing To Good Communication

Synopsisynopsis

To have a solid and sound marriage the vast majority would need to invest the proper measure of energy into the structure interaction.

This building system is typically a continuous exertion that ought not be underestimated at some random time.

It's Important

Focusing on great correspondence will likewise permit the couple to determine issues before they become wild issues. Great correspondence expertise will permit the two players to advance their singular perspectives without falling back on insidious measures like affronts and other negative verbal articulations.

Having the option to tweak the craft of commonly advantageous discussion will positively assist with setting up the couple for times when conflicts surface, as the past capacity to talk well, will assist with keeping the two of them zeroed in on settling the matter in the most genial manner.

Focusing on great correspondence will likewise assist the two players with investigating and track down appropriate arrangements as fast as conceivable rather than waiting on the issue.

In doing as such the issue can be contained and there is less possibilities of it raising and assuming control over the existences of the two players.

Wrapping Up

There are a few distinct reasons regarding the significance of focusing on having a decent and sound correspondence stage inside a marriage.

This is here and there the main method for keeping the marriage perfectly healthy, particularly assuming that one party can't so much for age or clinical motivations to enjoy any sexual action.

Having the option to have a decent discussion with one another is exceptionally reviving and edifying. This is significantly more significant as the marriage becomes older and there are no interruptions, for example, youngsters and tasks to possess their time.

In such occasions having the option to convey will and on a thrilling level will assist with keeping the marriage looking great.

Marriage is the most fragile and in a large portion of the cases most significant relationship known in this world.

Our life has become extremely unbending and occupied and this inflexible life has made loads of things turn out badly and one of the vital regions is marriage which gets impacted because of our undesirable, unsocial and at times silly living style. There are sure things that you really want to know and have to execute in your life and without these things you will be denied of that large number of cheerful snapshots of your life.

As indicated by an exploration proportion of separation and partition has expanded with time and there are vast purposes behind this expanded proportion.

In this EBook I will direct you towards making your marriage a better and blissful relationship.

You really want to realize that repairing your marriage is vital to carry on with a sound and prosperous life since I have seen individuals who screw up their marriage yet they not just screw their marriage rather when marriage is in a bad way then, at that point, everything in your life is in a bad way since it consequences for pretty much every field of your life. Whenever your marriage moves along as expected then, at that point, you feel extremely loose and there is just about no pressure in your life.

This less pressure expands your efficiency and permits you to focus more on your work rather than continuously pondering your relationship.

I have accumulated data from bunches of sources and afterward attempted to adjust everything up so you can have a superior comprehension of everything. Assuming you are contemplating getting into relationship of marriage or you are as of now running a marriage or regardless of whether you have a few inconveniences in your marriage then, at that point, you should continue to peruse this EBook and you will find solutions of pretty much every inquiry that comes to you.

Patching The Marriage

Fix The Holes Of Your Marriage And Experience The Feeling Of New Love

There are such countless obligations and changes that marriage gets your life and in this section, I will enlighten you concerning those responsibilities and changes.

Select your accomplice cautiously

Know yourself and know the other individual Living, cherishing and sharing ought to be there Be prepared to make a few changes and face a few inconveniences

The Basics

There are two sorts of day to day routines that all of us daily routines and these two lives are life as single and life as hitched individual.

There are heaps of contrasts in both of these lives that everybody needs to comprehend and on the off chance that you can't comprehend those distinctions and take both of these lives as same then, at that point, things will begin to get fastidious. Particularly when you don't change and don't adjust to wedded circumstances and you continue to stand up with those old single routine then, at that point, things can get undeniably challenging for your marriage.

There are sure things that you really want to know prior to reveling into your wedded life and following conversation will uncover those things.

Select Your Partner Carefully

First and most significant thing is to look and choose for the perfect individual who can go with you for the remainder of your life.

This can be vital as hellfire yet some of the time it turns out to be extremely simple task to take care of.

In both of the cases you ought to never hustle into a relationship and get to know one another before marriage. This will permit you to realize that how vastly different your characters are and the number of changes you should make to get by into that relationship. Assuming you can recognize that both of you are synchronizing with one another well and there are relatively few contrasts emerging during your relationship then, at that point, you can trust your faculties and move towards a better and more grounded wedded relationship however on the off chance that you are finding it hard to address that individual's disposition and you have a reasoning
that all will be great after marriage then, at that point, accept me nothing will be just after marriage since things can deteriorate after marriage.
Know Yourself and Know The Other Person

This is a significant angle which helps
you in picking the perfect individual.
As a matter of first importance, you
should know yourself appropriately
and know your restrictions, disposition
credits and comparable different
things and afterward attempt to search
for comparative kind of individual.
Realizing yourself implies that you
ought to be dependably show yourself
as you are to the next individual.
 It isn't unexpected seen that
individuals regularly untruth or make
things up while hoping to fabricate a
relationship yet this isn't the correct
method for getting it done.
Correspondingly realize the other
individual well by getting some
information about convictions and
other comparable things.
 These basic inquiries will lead you to a
more point by point comprehension of
that individual's demeanor and
potential issues with their disposition.

Living, Loving and Sharing Should Be There In the event that you are beginning another relationship, it is vital that you give the person in question legitimate opportunity to get you and this time ought incorporate gathering and eating together as well as there are such countless different things that you want to show to the next individual.

 On the off chance that affection and care are missing in those early days, you can never anticipate these things with the course of life.

These are exceptionally essential necessities of relationship and their nonattendance implies that the other individual is either not prepared to make a relationship or the person isn't very much created for being with you.

Attempt To Listen More Than Saying Listening is additionally one more vital part of connections and particularly when you are in beginning phase of your connections then, at that point, it is fundamental that you ought to pay attention to the next individual to know their perspectives about various parts of life.

 It isn't unexpected seen that individuals will generally talk more than tune in however you ought to be equivalent in both of these things and subsequent to making yourself clear once, pay attention to the next individual cautiously and attempt to realize that everything the person is attempting to say to you from their perspectives and talks.

Be Ready To Make Some Adjustments and Face Some Troubles

This is something perceived that at whatever point you are hoping to construct another relationship then, at that point, it will go through certain difficulties and issues however in the event that you began to freeze in these issues, things will deteriorate.

 These little inconveniences and contrasts will lead you to realize that how much tolerating the other individual is.

On the off chance that the individual is completely shaken with these issues, you should contemplate a few substitute choice and search for a superior individual yet you want to keep yourself made in these circumstances and attempt to ensure that the other individual isn't getting an articulation that you will make any penance for that relationship rather make a few little changes if necessary and cause her to accept that you are attempting to make everything work.
Fortifying Your Relationship Summation
In this part I will let you know a few significant things that can make your relationship more grounded and better.
Common obligation
Remember care for your relationship
Dispose of correspondence hole
Appropriate time for your relationship
Trust

Making It Stronger

In the above part you have realized every one of the significant things that are important to comprehend prior to making any relationship however presently we will move another above and beyond and I will let you know some critical that will tell you in the wake of making a relationship.

Making a responsibility or relationship is simple however it is exceptionally difficult to make that relationship work.

On the off chance that you don't know about a few essential fixings to work that relationship then, at that point, you will cut off up separating that friendship or either getting yourself lost in the intricacies of those relations.

It is particularly useful in spouse wife relationship that you need to take care for one another well and attempt to make your relationship work in a better way.

Common Responsibility

Obligation is the key in spouse wife relationship however certain individuals frequently misconstrue this obligation condition and think that husband is the only one liable for everything in this relationship.

This isn't the case on the grounds that the two accomplices are approached mindful in making the relationship work.

Assuming any of them imagines that the individual isn't mindful then things will begin to get terrible.

The sorts of liabilities are different for both of the accomplices.

Spouse's job is all the more a strong one while husband needs to deal with everything with care.

Little errors will constantly emerge however assuming that you are adequately dependable to acknowledge your shortcoming then, at that point, these misconception will make your relationship considerably more grounded.

Remember Care for Your Relationship
This is human instinct that we generally love to get care.
 This is valid in spouse wife relationship in light of the fact that the more you care for one another, more grounded will turn into your relationship.
 Care is likewise a common activity since, in such a case that you are not really focusing on the other accomplice then, at that point, the individual will likewise not try to think often about you.
Care isn't something extremely hard and exact thing that you can't do rather there are a few tiny things remembered for this consideration. For instance assuming you can simply give an additional a call to your significant other for asking her that how she is feeling and for telling her that you generally recollect her, will make it a tremendous motion for your better half.

Comparably in the event that you are a spouse, simply a mitigating grin to your significant other, when he returns home following a tiring day in office, is to the point of causing him to accept that you generally care for him. You can think of it as similarly as a passionate ledger and you need to store all the nice sentiment, better motions and caring words in that financial balance.

 On the off chance that you don't store enough of this stuff in that passionate ledger then, at that point, you can anticipate nothing consequently.

Dispose Of Communication Gap

Correspondence hole is another vital component that can make your relationship more fragile.
In new connections correspondence is the key and without appropriate correspondence you can not let your accomplice know that the amount you care for the person in question neither one of the you will actually want to let them know that what sort of mentality you have.
 On the off chance that you tell less, eventually you will likewise know less. To realize the other individual well, you should talk a ton and attempt to know all that you would be able.
 It isn't required that you ought to get some information about a few extremely significant and large issues however you can begin from exceptionally ordinary and agreeable conversations and afterward progress onto a few more complicated issues of life.

A lot talking and exceptionally less listening is likewise not extremely smart for connections in light of the fact that in that way you can not have the foggiest idea about the other individual quite well.

The most ideal way to impart and realize the other individual is to clear yourself totally and afterward pay attention to the next individual cautiously.

This expanded correspondence won't just assistance you in making the relationship more grounded however it additionally helps you in diminishing the misconceptions all the more successfully in light of the fact that at whatever point something turns out badly with your relationship then, at that point, you can talk our beginning and end and matter can be tackled cautiously.

Legitimate Time for Your Relationship Timing is likewise vital and you want to ensure that you are giving sufficient opportunity to your relationship.

Indeed less time assignment to relationship is the significant explanation of separations nowadays. Life is exceptionally bustling nowadays and a large portion of individuals work all day, every day to make due and to meet their living norms in this general public however in this battle of bringing in cash, connections are frequently disregarded and individuals experience the ill effects of separations.

On the off chance that you are a spouse or an acquiring wife, you ought to examine your week by week timetable and attempt to confirm that how long you are providing for your family and your accomplice.

This examination will let you know that the amount you want to chip away at your relationship and the amount additional time you want to provide for your relationship timing likewise incorporates that you should get out from under that old daily practice and propensity for 9-5 a few times.

Get a component of shock your relationship and get back home from your office early once in a while.

This little signal will cost you only will make your accomplice extremely blissful and the person will feel that you care for them.

Trust Trust is another vital thing and you can say that it is likewise one of the shared sentiments that you really want to create between your connections.

In the event that you don't believe your accomplice then, at that point, you can't anticipate that your accomplice should trust you.

Trust does likewise not just about accept that your accomplice will not modest upon you yet it additionally implies that you should realize that your accomplice can never conflict with their obligations connected with that relationship.

All of the previously mentioned things are extremely simple to execute in your day to day routine and they incorporate nothing that is exceptionally intricate and on the off chance that you truly do minimal additional attempt, these things can make your connections exceptionally solid and sound.

Great connections and strain free connections can likewise improve your real life since pressure is unsafe all the time for wellbeing.

Control and Make Your Marriage Concrete

Summary In this section, you will know that large number of significant things that can lead you to a more grounded and controlled marriage.

Make a few principles and follow them

Helping one another Never let the sentiment kick the bucket from your relationship

Monetary security

Make It Stable
Mistaken assumptions and miscommunications are exceptionally normal things in the present relationships and the vast majority of these things come due to misusing of this relationship.
 You should realize that spouse wife relationship is exceptionally fragile relationship that requirements loads of care and consideration from the two players to remain on the way. Following conversation will let you know that what are those essential necessities that you want to satisfy for a far reaching and more grounded marriage.
Make Some Rules and Follow Them
Living short of what one rooftop can be intense on occasion and particularly when you return from various grounds then, at that point, it turns out to be much harder to adapt to that large number of contrasts that you have

incorporated in one another's characters.

There is straightforward strategy that can help you in living with no difficulties.

You really want to make a few principles in the house and afterward ensure that you both keep those guidelines.

It isn't unexpected seen that spouse and wives don't will generally let each know other their preferences yet things can be parcel more straightforward and less difficult assuming you can simply say your perspective in open.

For instance as opposed to sitting calm in the secondary lounge and gnawing your nails, you can simply let your accomplice know that he should drive under or not exactly explicit speed on the grounds that expecting that he will know what you need won't get that going.

Correspondingly there can be so many other basic guidelines that you can make and these principles, whenever followed appropriately can save you from heaps of errors.

Helping Each Other

Whenever you live under one rooftop then, at that point, there are sure liabilities that you both need to satisfy.

In the event that you are spouse, you will undoubtedly assist your protected in day by day families and particularly on ends of the week you with expecting to ensure that you are with your better half in nearly everything since she likewise needs rest and you're almost no assist with willing give an extremely incredible inclination to her. Comparatively on the off chance that you are a spouse, it is your obligation that you should make your significant other as agreeable as possible. In the event that you welcome your significant other home with an adorable grin, it will improve

78

everything and your better half will get an inclination that his entire day's worth of effort is all around spent yet assuming you begin hollering at your significant other just after his entry in the house then, at that point, it will begin to build the pressure and your better half won't be truly alright with that.

Never Let the Romance Die From Your Relationship

Whenever you have invested some energy with your accomplice then, at that point, the majority of the times it happens that your relationship become unsurprising and everything becomes known.

Indeed, even individuals add sentiment in that anticipated nature however this isn't the right way to deal with embrace rather you should attempt to keep sentiment alive all through your relationship.

Sentiment isn't just about

having intercourse in the bed however there are so many thing that can make your relationship more heartfelt.

On the off chance that you are coming from the workplace and you see a bloom shop on the manner in which then, at that point, bringing a straightforward blossom pail is likewise remembered for sentiment and this little and practically modest signal can make your life exceptionally heartfelt and can make an extremely charming inclination about you in the core of your accomplice.

So continue to do comparable signals to keep sentiment alive in your relationship.

Monetary Stability

Monetary soundness is something else that prompts a dependable relationship in light of the fact that monetary security gives you truly stable spot in the public eye and diminishes loads of your pressure and every day strains. Certain individuals whine that their spouses don't give them support in terrible monetary circumstances however this isn't the case except if you are too apathetic to even think about changing your monetary status. In the event that you are genuine with the reason and making an honest effort to improve in life then, at that point, there is no young lady in this world who won't remain with you in difficult situations however issues start when you quit going after for something good.

Continuously offer you most obvious opportunity and afterward, you can anticipate support for your accomplice. Comparable is the situation with spouse that of she sees that her significant other can't satisfy every one of the monetary necessities of the family then, at that point, she should work and support her better half all around that she would be able.

In this part I will let you know a few insider facts tips that can get you out of the difficulties, assuming you have any in your marriage.

 Continuously think positive and acknowledge the obligation

 Unlimited satisfaction In the event that you need your accomplice to change, change yourself first

 Absolution can make your relationship more concrete and strong

 Otherworldliness can get congruity and unobtrusiveness your relationship Get Along As a wedded couple, it is an alternate everyday routine by and large that you need to experience. There are heaps of compromises that you need to make and simultaneously, there are loads of things that you generally need to do without wanting to however all of this is for the greater advantages of your future.

Assuming you can make a few slight trade offs to make your approaching life more straightforward and better then, at that point, there is nothing out of sorts in that and you ought to never embed your inner self in these issues. In the above conversations, I have let you know that how you can choose your ideal accomplice and afterward I let you know that what are the things that can make your marriage more compelling and longer enduring? In this conversation I will educate you concerning a few things and systems that you can take on if there should be an occurrence of any misconception or any disarray that has occurred in your relationship.

Continuously Think Positive and Accept The Responsibility

This is something perceived that while a misconception happens then, at that point, it isn't from one side in particular and the two accomplices hold equivalent offers in that battle. This is a reality that not many individuals can acknowledge in light of the fact that everybody begins to look for someone else to take the blame and nobody acknowledges their issues.

 This demeanor ought to be adjusted and you should be valiant enough that you should say alright I did or said this wrong and I am upset for that. Whenever you have said and understood that shortcoming or slip-up was on your end then, at that point, it becomes more straightforward for the other individual to acknowledge their issue as well.

you should be certain about your relationship and never contemplate separating the relationship rather consistently search for an exit plan.

Unequivocal Happiness

Certain individuals partner bliss with specific things like on the off chance that they will take some time off, they will be more joyful however residing in home is dull and exhausting for them. This should be not the case since life is brimming with satisfaction and you really want to simply look through

84

more modest however truly charming snapshots of life in day to day existence.

 For instance when you play b-ball with your child then, at that point, it likewise should give some joy. Correspondingly when your little girl helps you out first time in the kitchen then, at that point, it ought to likewise give joy for yourself and comparative other more modest things.

Nowadays' kin regularly disregard these more modest cheerful minutes and they are continuously searching for a few major events and this disposition is likewise not exceptionally accommodating for relationship and makes pressure and strain.

On the off chance that You Want Your Partner to Change, Change Yourself First Certain individuals generally need to coordinate a few novel things in their lives and these remarkable things become truly challenging to incorporate in the existences of other individual.

This isn't the correct method for transforming somebody rather you want to start change from yourself and bring a few changes that your accomplice likes. Whenever you will get those changes your character then, at that point, your accomplice will be naturally inspired to transform oneself since the individual in question will realize that you have regarded their thoughts and changed yourself so presently it turns into their obligation to bring Pardoning Can Make Your Relationship More Concrete And Invincible As I have referenced over that life has become extremely intense nowadays and there isn't a lot of chance to take care of one another.

This bustling life has additionally removed pardoning and resilience from this general public and any place you see, there is what is happening like mayhem and outrageous pressure.

Nobody is prepared to pardon even the littlest of error of others.

 In the event that you additionally have that sort of unforgiving disposition, you want to transform it for more prominent reason and to make your relationship more concrete. Pardoning consistently assists with building connections and when you excuse little mix-ups of your accomplice then, at that point, the person in question begins to regard you more and more modest false impressions can never break your relationship.

Otherworldliness Can Bring Harmony and Modesty in Your Relationship

Our life has become an excessive amount of materialistic and there is next to no edge of otherworldliness accessible.

To practice otherworldliness, it isn't required for you to have confidence in a specific religion yet you simply should be extremely straight with regards to your viewpoints and attempt

87

to make your life smoother by rehearsing some psyche cooling works out.

These activities can help you a great deal in achieving the smoothness and humility in your methodology towards relationship.

Instructions to Avoid Break Ups

Abstract In this section I will let you know a few hints that you can apply and stay away from any separations in your connections.

 Know the family distinctions

 Give appropriate chance to your relationship

 Everyday reassurance is significant

 Settle on a truce is the smartest strategy

 Explain things and afterward pay attention to the next individual

 Continuously be on the point in your false impressions

Remain Strong

Conflicts are essential for connections however these conflicts ought to never break your connections and you should track down an exit plan.

Indeed, even a few conflicts can make your relationship more grounded it could be said that they allow you an opportunity to know one another better.

Following are a few hints that you want to follow and you can keep away from a wide range of conflicts and separations.

Know the Family Differences

There can be heaps of issues in your new connections however to tackle that issue you really want to comprehend the family distinctions. There can be loads of various examples and customs in both of your families and to take on these practices and family designs you should do a few trade offs. This is likewise a shared agreement that you need to take on and both the accomplices are expected to take an interest in this setting effectively.

Give Proper Time to Your Relationship

Timing is additionally significant in each relationship and particularly when you are in another relationship then, at that point, it is important to give legitimate chance to your relationship. Life can be extremely occupied and particularly nowadays you need to strive to meet your day by day needs yet connections generally need care and time.

 You likewise need to break that normal that creates with time. Continuously have a component of shock in your day to day routine. Regardless of whether you have met some battle or misjudging then, at that point, you should give each other some time to get comfortable.

 on the off chance that you begin to put forth attempts to determine everything just after the battle then, at that point, it could exacerbate the situation.

Everyday encouragement Is Important

Everyday encouragement implies that

you want to acknowledge the distinctions that you have in one another's lives.

There is a truism that you really want to settle on a truce.

This maxim is extremely evident and exceptionally substantial that you need to execute in your every day relationship.

You likewise need to give some help to your accomplice and acknowledge about their position cautiously.

You really want to comprehend that changes ought to be produced using the two closures.

You should assume your part while permit the other accomplice to assume their part.

Settle on a truce Is the Best Policy

Here can be two circumstances in your day to day existence, regardless of whether you can have a battle or separate and you won't ever need a fix up however there can be an alternate circumstance in which you can be tingling to fix up.

91

In that circumstance you ought to settle on a truce and acknowledge your deficiencies.
This can be the most straightforward arrangement of your concerns and is likewise extremely powerful.
I have seen individuals that become survivor of their self images and they never acknowledge that there is anything amiss with them rather they continue to look for someone else to take the blame that compounds the situation for them.
Keep away from that disposition and foster a tolerant and capable demeanor to save your relationchip Explain Things and afterward Listen To The Other Person This is another generally observed issue that while some misconception occurs between the couple then, at that point, both of the accomplices don't pay attention to one another and they continue to tell their place of perspectives independently. This isn't the right methodology and it

won't ever tackle your concerns rather you want to embrace a methodology of doing all that unmistakable once and afterward begin to pay attention to the next accomplice.

This will permit you to clear your front and furthermore stand by listening to the next individual and it can make things lit better and more obvious.

To put it plainly, you can say that you should be an excellent audience and apply those listening abilities in your relationship.

Continuously Be On the Point In Your Misunderstandings

This is another exceptionally normal error that the vast majority of the couples make that they start attempt at finger pointing and when some misconception is grown then, at that point, they continue bringing everything from past in that misconception.

This ought to be kept away from in light of the fact that it makes things complex and you ought to be dependably on the money about a specific misconception.

Try not to wander from the center issue and attempt to determine it as one issue rather than blending all the previous issues in it and befuddling each other with regards to the arrangement.

A few General Secrets and Trends for Improving Your Marital Relationship Outline In this section I will let you know a few more definite and more broad arrangements that can help you in retouching your marriage.

Knowing one another realle Try not to be excessively frantic Comprehend other individual's point of view Make liability of your words and moves completely Become along with time

Accept and trust are the keys to effective marriag On the off chance that you are hitched and searching for counsel, the previously mentioned tips and techniques can truly assist you in saving your marriage and you with canning make your marriage an extremely amazing connection between two spirits.

There are a few other significant things additionally there that can truly help you in being valid perfect partners.

Following are those excess things that can assist you with making your relationship more concrete and sound. Knowing Each Other Truly I have referenced this point above likewise that knowing one another is vital and particularly when you need to carry on with the remainder of the coexistence then, at that point, it turns out to be vital that you should know every one of the perspectives and considerations of one another pretty much every one of the various things and situations.

In that course of realizing each other you should be totally ready to confront the showdowns and conflicts and yet yo9u should be extremely unassuming as you will be tested with regards to your perspectives and will be given a few unique decisions to embrace.

You ought to dissect those decisions decidedly and contemplate all perspectives.

 In the event that a few ideas are possible, acknowledge them with an open heart.

Try not to Be Too Desperate These days the vast majority of individuals come from broken families and the present circumstance makes them extremely frantic now and again that they settle on off-base decisions looking for a family.

 This is valid that you ought to continuously search for a superior life however in that battle you ought not fail to remember that there is your own life likewise at stack and an off-base decision about your accomplice or comparable other decision can demolish for what seems like forever. Take as much time as necessary and settle on decision after some examination and as referenced above in the wake of knowing one another well.

Comprehend Other Person's Perspective It is exceptionally hard on occasion to comprehend other individual's viewpoint about various things however this is extremely pivotal too in light of the fact that without coming to at the specific degree of other individual, you can not convey and tell the person in question precisely the way in which you feel.

To ensure that you have gotten everything and entire character of other individual you really want to see things from his eyes and attempt to think in the manner the person in question thinks.

This will permit you to convey your own thought all the more plainly too in light of the fact that when you will begin understanding him then, at that point, you will actually want to take on those ways which are more advantageous and nearer to his methodology and his contemplations.

Make Responsibility of Your Words And Moves Thoroughly I have portrayed this reality all through this EBook and it is vital too that you should be liable for your own behavior words and comparable different signals.

You really want to quit faulting each other for shortcomings and misconstruing and set yourself up to make a portion of the move on you. This will make the connection simpler and you will actually want to tackle a large number issues without any problem.

Particularly when both of the people will acknowledge their disparities then, at that point, it truly turns into a smooth ride out and out.

Become Together With Time This is additionally exceptionally pivotal piece of any relationship that individuals generally anticipate that the other individual should stay same even following 5 or 10 years have passed however this should be not the methodology since time changes heaps of things and comparative is the situation with characters.

You want to acknowledge those changes and truth be told you want to

invite those changes that accompany
time.

In the event that you begin opposing to
those changes, things will get extreme
for the other individual and the person
in question will likewise oppose to your
changes. So to secure and thrive your
connections never acknowledge your
accomplice to stay same all through
the life.

Accept And Trust Are the Keys To
Successful Marriage Accept and trusts
are two of the achievements for
building an effective conjugal
relationship.

On the off chance that these two things
are available, your life can be a walk in
the park while their nonappearance
can make your life harder than you
envisioned.

Both of these sentiments are common
and when one accomplice begins to
believe the other then, at that point,
other will likewise regard and believe
you.

This is human instinct that in the
event that spouse checks the wireless

and call record of husband, husband will likewise keep an eye on his better half. To stay away from such circumstances, you should keep trust and accept as the impetus for your relationship.

Wrapping up In the above EBook I have attempted to let you know pretty much every significant thing that can make your marriage work and I am 100% certain that regardless of whether you execute 50% of the above things in your relationship then, at that point, you can never anticipate a disappointment.

All of the above data is exceptionally obvious and is removed from many genuine encounters. Long exploration is been done behind this EBook and I have attempted to let you know every one of the concentrates of that examination.

Marriage is a hard period of the life and particularly in start since you are appended with somebody whom you only know for one or 2 years and you need to go through entire of your time on earth with that individual. It appears to be an exceptionally predicament and the greater part of individuals alarm when they get into this relationship however on the off chance that you keep your nerves in charge and be unobtrusive and quiet in your methodology then, at that point, it very well may be an extremely worth investing energy of your life.